THE YOGA OF DIVINE LOVE...

A world-renowned *yoga* master cuts through the commercialism that now clouds the real meaning of *yoga*.

His Divine Grace A.C. Bhaktivedanta Swami Prabhupāda explains that beyond the postures and exercises, the ancient teachings of *yoga* aim at lasting, loving union with the Supreme.

Books by His Divine Grace A.C. Bhaktivedanta Swami Prabhupāda

Bhagavad-gītā As It Is
Śrīmad-Bhāgavatam (completed by disciples)
Śrī Caitanya-caritāmṛta
Kṛṣṇa, the Supreme Personality of Godhead
Teachings of Lord Caitanya
The Nectar of Devotion
The Nectar of Instruction
Śrī Īśopaniṣad
Light of the Bhāgavata
Easy Journey to Other Planets
Teachings of Lord Kapila, the Son of Devahūti
Teachings of Queen Kuntī
Message of Godhead
The Science of Self-Realization
The Perfection of Yoga
Beyond Birth and Death
On the Way to Kṛṣṇa
Rāja-vidyā: The King of Knowledge
Elevation to Kṛṣṇa Consciousness
Kṛṣṇa Consciousness: The Matchless Gift
Kṛṣṇa Consciousness: The Topmost Yoga System
Perfect Questions, Perfect Answers
Life Comes from Life
The Nārada-bhakti-sūtra (completed by disciples)
The Mukunda-mālā-stotra (completed by disciples)
Geetār-gan (Bengali)
Vairāgya-vidyā (Bengali)
Buddhi-yoga (Bengali)
Bhakti-ratna-boli (Bengali)
Back to Godhead magazine (founder)

Books compiled from the teachings of His Divine Grace A.C. Bhaktivedanta Swami Prabhupāda after his lifetime

Search for Liberation
A Second Chance
The Journey of Self-Discovery
Civilization and Transcendence
The Laws of Nature
Renunciation Through Wisdom
The Quest for Enlightenment
Dharma, the Way of Transcendence
Beyond Illusion and Doubt
The Hare Kṛṣṇa Challenge

Available from: www.krishna.com

ALL GLORY TO ŚRĪ GŪRŪ AND GAURĀṄGA

THE PERFECTION OF *yoga*

His Divine Grace
A.C. Bhaktivedanta Swami Prabhupāda
Founder-*Ācārya* of the International Society for Krishna Consciousness

THE BHAKTIVEDANTA BOOK TRUST

Readers interested in the subject matter of this book are invited by the International Society for Krishna Consciousness to visit any ISKCON center (see address list in back of book) or to correspond with the Secretary.

ISKCON Reader Services
P.O. Box 730, Watford, WD25 8ZE, United Kingdom
Tel: +44 (0)1923 857244 • readerservices@pamho.net
www.iskcon.org.uk

Karuna Bhavan
Bankhouse Rd., Lesmahagow,Lanarkshire, ML11 0ES, Scotland
Tel: +44 (0)1555 894790 • Fax: +44 (0)1555 894526
karunabhavan@aol.com • www.iskcon.org.uk/scotland

ISKCON
83 Middle Abbey Street, Dublin 1, Republic of Ireland
Tel: +353 (0)1 8729775 • mail@krishna.ie • www.krishna.ie

The Perfection of Yoga was prepared from transcripts of lectures Śrīla Prabhupāda gave in 1966 and 1969 on the sixth chapter of the *Bhagavad-gītā*. The editor was Śrīla Prabhupāda's disciple Hayagrīva Dāsa (Howard Wheeler, MA). It was first published in 1972.

FSC
Mixed Sources
Product group from well-managed forests and other controlled sources

Cert no. SGS-COC-1940
www.fsc.org
© 1996 Forest Stewardship Council

The FSC-certified stock *Holmen Book Cream* was produced by Holmen Paper in Hallsta, Sweden.

Printed in 2008
978-1-84599-040-4

www.krishna.com
www.bbt.info

Contents

ONE

Yoga as Rejected by Arjuna

THERE HAVE BEEN many *yoga* systems popularized in the Western world, especially in this century, but none of them have actually taught the perfection of *yoga*. In the *Bhagavad-gītā,* Śrī Kṛṣṇa, the Supreme Personality of Godhead, teaches Arjuna directly the perfection of *yoga*. If we actually want to participate in the perfection of the *yoga* system, in *Bhagavad-gītā* we will find the authoritative statements of the Supreme Person.

It is certainly remarkable that the perfection of *yoga* was taught in the middle of a battlefield. It was taught to Arjuna, the warrior, just before Arjuna was to engage in a fratricidal battle. Out of sentiment, Arjuna was thinking, "Why should I fight against my own kinsmen?" That reluctance to fight was due to Arjuna's illusion, and just to eradicate that illusion, Śrī Kṛṣṇa spoke the *Bhagavad-gītā* to him. One can just imagine how little time must have elapsed while *Bhagavad-gītā* was being spoken. All the warriors on both sides were poised to fight, so there was very little time indeed—at the utmost, one hour. Within this one hour, the whole *Bhagavad-gītā* was discussed, and Śrī Kṛṣṇa set forth the perfection of all *yoga* systems to His friend Arjuna. At the end of this great discourse, Arjuna set aside his misgivings and fought.

However, within the discourse, when Arjuna heard the explanation of the meditational system of *yoga*—how to sit down, how to keep the body straight, how to keep the eyes half-closed and how to gaze at the tip of the nose without diverting one's attention, all this being conducted in a secluded place, alone—he replied,

yo 'yaṁ yogas tvayā proktaḥ
sāmyena madhusūdana
etasyāhaṁ na paśyāmi
cañcalatvāt sthitiṁ sthirām

"O Madhusūdana, the system of *yoga* which You have summarized appears impractical and unendurable to me, for the mind is restless and unsteady." (Bg. 6.33) This is important. We must always remember that we are in a material circumstance wherein at every moment our mind is subject to agitation. Actually we are not in a very comfortable situation. We are always thinking that by changing our situation we will overcome our mental agitation, and we are always thinking that when we reach a certain point, all mental agitations will disappear. But it is the nature of the material world that we cannot be free from anxiety. Our dilemma is that we are always trying to make a solution to our problems, but this universe is so designed that these solutions never come.

Not being a cheater, being very frank and open, Arjuna tells Kṛṣṇa that the system of *yoga* which He has described is not possible for him to execute. In speaking to Kṛṣṇa, it is significant that Arjuna addresses Him as Madhusūdana, indicating that the Lord is the killer of the demon Madhu. It is notable that God's names are innumerable, for He is often named according to His activities. Indeed, God has innumerable names because He has innumerable activities. We are only parts of God, and we cannot even remember how many activities we have engaged in from our childhood to the present. The eternal God is unlimited, and since His activities are also unlimited, He has unlimited names, of which *Kṛṣṇa* is the chief. Then why is Arjuna addressing Him as Madhusūdana when, being Kṛṣṇa's friend, he could address Him directly as Kṛṣṇa? The answer is that Arjuna considers his mind to be like a great demon, such as the demon Madhu. If it were possible for Kṛṣṇa to kill the demon called the mind, then Arjuna would be able to attain the perfection of *yoga*. "My mind is much stronger than this demon Madhu," Arjuna is saying. "Please, if You could kill him, then it would be possible for me to execute this *yoga* system." Even the mind of a great man like Arjuna is always agitated. As Arjuna himself says,

cañcalaṁ hi manaḥ kṛṣṇa
pramāthi balavad dṛḍham
tasyāhaṁ nigrahaṁ manye
vāyor iva suduṣkaram

"For the mind is restless, turbulent, obstinate and very strong, O Kṛṣṇa, and to subdue it is, it seems to me, more difficult than controlling the wind." (Bg. 6.34)

It is indeed a fact that the mind is always telling us to go here, go there, do this, do that—it is always telling us which way to turn. Thus the sum and substance of the *yoga* system is to control the agitated mind. In the meditational *yoga* system the mind is controlled by focusing on the Supersoul—that is the whole purpose of *yoga*. But Arjuna says that controlling this mind is more difficult than stopping the wind from blowing. One can imagine a man stretching out his arms trying to stop a hurricane. Are we to assume that Arjuna is simply not sufficiently qualified to control his mind? The actual fact is that we cannot begin to understand the immense qualifications of Arjuna. After all, he was a personal friend of the Supreme Personality of Godhead. This is a highly elevated position and is one that cannot be at all attained by one without great qualifications. In addition to this, Arjuna was renowned as a great warrior and administrator. He was such an intelligent man that he could understand *Bhagavad-gītā* within one hour, whereas at the present moment great scholars cannot even understand it in the course of a lifetime. Yet Arjuna was thinking that controlling the mind was simply not possible for him. Are we then to assume that what was impossible for Arjuna in a more advanced age is possible for us in this degenerate age? We should not for one moment think that we are in Arjuna's category. We are a thousand times inferior.

Moreover, there is no record of Arjuna's having executed the *yoga* system at any time. Yet Arjuna was praised by Kṛṣṇa as the only man worthy of understanding *Bhagavad-gītā*. What was Arjuna's great qualification? Śrī Kṛṣṇa says, "You are My devotee. You are My very dear friend." Despite this qualification, Arjuna refused to execute the meditational *yoga* system described by Śrī Kṛṣṇa. What then are we to conclude? Are we to despair the mind's ever being controlled? No, it can be controlled, and the process is this Kṛṣṇa consciousness. The mind must be fixed always in Kṛṣṇa. Insofar as the mind is absorbed in Kṛṣṇa, it has attained the perfection of *yoga*.

Now when we turn to the *Śrīmad-Bhāgavatam,* in the Twelfth Canto we find Śukadeva Gosvāmī telling Mahārāja Parīkṣit that in the golden age, the Satya-yuga, people were living for one hundred thousand years, and at that time, when advanced living entities lived for such lengths of time, it was possible to execute this meditational system of *yoga*. But what was achieved in the Satya-yuga by this meditational process, and in the following *yuga,* the Tretā-yuga, by the offering of great sacrifices, and in the next *yuga,* the Dvāpara-yuga, by temple worship, would be achieved at the present time, in this Kali-yuga, by simply chanting the names of God, *hari-kīrtana,* Hare Kṛṣṇa. So from authoritative sources we learn that this chanting of Hare Kṛṣṇa, Hare Kṛṣṇa, Kṛṣṇa Kṛṣṇa, Hare Hare/ Hare Rāma, Hare Rāma, Rāma Rāma, Hare Hare is the embodiment of the perfection of *yoga* for this age.

Today we have great difficulties living fifty or sixty years. A man may live at the utmost eighty or a hundred years. In addition, these brief years are always fraught with anxiety, with difficulties due to circumstances of war, pestilence, famine and so many other disturbances. We're also not very intelligent, and, at the same time, we're unfortunate. These are the characteristics of man living in Kali-yuga, a degraded age. So properly speaking, we can never attain success in this meditational *yoga* system described by Kṛṣṇa. At the utmost we can only gratify our personal whims by some pseudoadaptation of this system. Thus people are paying money to attend some classes in gymnastic exercises and deep-breathing, and they're happy if they think they can lengthen their lifetimes by a few years or enjoy better sex life. But we must understand that this is not the actual *yoga* system. In this age that meditational system cannot be properly executed. Instead, all of the perfections of that system can be realized through *bhakti-yoga,* the sublime process of Kṛṣṇa consciousness, specifically *mantra-yoga,* the glorification of Śrī Kṛṣṇa through the chanting of Hare Kṛṣṇa. That is recommended in Vedic scriptures and is introduced by great authorities like Caitanya Mahāprabhu. Indeed, the *Bhagavad-gītā* proclaims that the *mahātmās,* the great souls, are always chanting the glories of the Lord. If one wants to be a *mahātmā* in terms of the Vedic literature, in terms of *Bhagavad-gītā* and in terms of the great authorities, then one has to adopt this process of Kṛṣṇa consciousness and of chanting Hare Kṛṣṇa. But if we're content at making a show of meditation by sitting very straight in lotus position and going into a trance like some sort of performer, then that is a different thing. But we should understand that such show-bottle performances have nothing to do with the actual perfection of *yoga.* The material disease cannot be cured by artificial medicine. We have to take the real cure straight from Kṛṣṇa.

TWO

Yoga as Work in Devotion

WE HAVE HEARD the names of so many different *yogas* and *yogīs*, but in *Bhagavad-gītā* Kṛṣṇa says that the actual *yogī* is he who has surrendered himself "fully unto Me." Kṛṣṇa proclaims that there is no difference between renunciation (*sannyāsa*) and *yoga*.

yaṁ sannyāsam iti prāhur
yogaṁ taṁ viddhi pāṇḍava
na hy asannyasta-saṅkalpo
yogī bhavati kaścana

"What is called renunciation is the same as *yoga*, or linking oneself with the Supreme; for no one can become a *yogī* unless he renounces the desire for sense gratification." (Bg. 6.2)

In *Bhagavad-gītā* there are three basic types of *yoga* delineated—*karma-yoga*, *jñāna-yoga* and *bhakti-yoga*. The systems of *yoga* may be likened to a staircase. Someone may be on the first step, someone may be halfway up, or someone may be on the top step. When one is elevated to certain levels, he is known as a *karma-yogī, jñāna-yogī,* etc. In all cases, the service to the Supreme Lord is the same. It is a difference in elevation only. Thus Śrī Kṛṣṇa tells Arjuna that he must understand that renunciation (*sannyāsa*) and *yoga* are the same, because without being freed from desire and sense gratification one can become neither a *yogī* nor a *sannyāsī.*

There are some *yogīs* who perform *yoga* for a profit, but that is not real *yoga.* Everything must be engaged in the service of the Lord. Whatever we do as an ordinary worker or as a *sannyāsī* or as a *yogī* or as a philosopher must be done in Kṛṣṇa consciousness. When we are absorbed in the thought of serving Kṛṣṇa and when we act in that consciousness, we can become real *sannyāsīs* and real *yogīs.* For those who are taking the first step up the staircase of the *yoga* system, there is work. One should not think that simply because he is beginning *yoga* he should stop working. In *Bhagavad-gītā* Kṛṣṇa asks Arjuna to become a *yogī,* but He never tells him to cease from fighting. Quite the contrary. Of course, one may ask how a person may be a *yogī* and at the same time a warrior. Our conception of *yoga* practice is that of sitting very straight, with legs crossed and eyes half-closed, staring at the tip of our nose and concentrating in this way in a lonely place. So how is it that Kṛṣṇa is asking Arjuna to become a *yogī* and at the same time participate in a ghastly civil war? That is the mystery of *Bhagavad-gītā:* one can remain a fighting man and at the same time be the highest *yogī,* the highest *sannyāsī.* How is this possible? In Kṛṣṇa consciousness. One simply has to fight for Kṛṣṇa, work for Kṛṣṇa, eat for Kṛṣṇa, sleep for Kṛṣṇa and dedicate all activities to Kṛṣṇa. In this way one becomes the highest *yogī* and the highest *sannyāsī.* That is the secret.

In the Sixth Chapter of *Bhagavad-gītā*, Śrī Kṛṣṇa instructs Arjuna how to perform meditational *yoga,* but Arjuna rejects this as too difficult. How then is Arjuna considered to be a great *yogī*? Although Kṛṣṇa saw that Arjuna was rejecting the meditational system, He proclaimed Arjuna to be the highest *yogī* because "You are always thinking of Me." Thinking of Kṛṣṇa is the essence of all *yoga* systems—of the *haṭha, karma, jñāna, bhakti* or any other system of *yoga,* sacrifice or charity. All the recommended activities for spiritual realization end in Kṛṣṇa consciousness, in thinking always of Kṛṣṇa. The actual perfection of human life lies in being always Kṛṣṇa conscious and always being aware of Kṛṣṇa while performing all types of activities.

In the preliminary stage one is advised to always work for Kṛṣṇa. One must be always searching out some duty or some engagement, for it is a bad policy to remain idle even for a second. When one actually becomes advanced through such engagements, then he may not work physically, but he is always engaged within by constantly thinking of Kṛṣṇa. In the preliminary stage, however, one is always advised to engage one's senses in the service of Kṛṣṇa. There are a variety of activities one can perform in serving Kṛṣṇa. The International Society for Krishna Consciousness is intended to help direct aspirant devotees in these activities. For those working in Kṛṣṇa consciousness, there are simply not enough hours in the day to serve Kṛṣṇa. There are always activities, engagements both day and night, which the student of Kṛṣṇa consciousness performs joyfully. That is the stage of real happiness—constant engagement for Kṛṣṇa and spreading Kṛṣṇa consciousness around the world. In the material world one may become very tired if he works all the time, but if one works in Kṛṣṇa consciousness, he can chant Hare Kṛṣṇa and engage in devotional service twenty-four hours a day and never get tired. But if we vibrate some mundane vibration, then we soon become exhausted. There is no question of becoming tired on the spiritual platform. The spiritual platform is absolute. In the material world everyone is working for sense gratification. The profits of one's labour in the material world are used to gratify one's senses. But a real *yogī* does not desire such fruits. He has no desire other than Kṛṣṇa, and Kṛṣṇa is already there.

THREE

Yoga as Meditation on Kṛṣṇa

IN INDIA there are sacred places where *yogīs* go to meditate in solitude, as prescribed in *Bhagavad-gītā.* Traditionally, *yoga* cannot be executed in a public place, but insofar as *kīrtana—mantra-yoga,* or the *yoga* of chanting the Hare Kṛṣṇa *mantra:* Hare Kṛṣṇa, Hare Kṛṣṇa, Kṛṣṇa Kṛṣṇa, Hare Hare/ Hare Rāma, Hare Rāma, Rāma Rāma, Hare Hare—is concerned, the more people present, the better. When Lord Caitanya Mahāprabhu was performing *kīrtana* in India some five hundred years ago, He organized in each group sixteen people to lead the chanting, and thousands of people chanted with them. This participation in *kīrtana,* in the public chanting of the names and glories of God, is very possible and is actually easy in this age; but as far as the meditational process of *yoga* is concerned, that is very difficult. It is specifically stated in *Bhagavad-gītā* that to perform meditational *yoga* one should go to a secluded and holy place. In other words, it is necessary to leave home. In this age of overpopulation it is not always possible to find a secluded place, but this is not necessary in *bhakti-yoga*.

In the *bhakti-yoga* system there are nine different processes: hearing, chanting, remembering, serving, worshiping the Deity in the temple, praying, carrying out orders, serving Kṛṣṇa as a friend and sacrificing for Him. Out of these, *śravaṇaṁ kīrtanam*, hearing and chanting, are considered the most important. At a public *kīrtana* one person can chant Hare Kṛṣṇa, Hare Kṛṣṇa, Kṛṣṇa Kṛṣṇa, Hare Hare/ Hare Rāma, Hare Rāma, Rāma Rāma, Hare Hare, while a group listens, and at the end of the *mantra*, the group can respond, and in this way there is a reciprocation of hearing and chanting. This can easily be performed in one's own home, with a small group of friends or with many people in a large public place. One may attempt to practice meditational *yoga* in a large city or in a society, but one must understand that this is one's own concoction and is not the method recommended in *Bhagavad-gītā*.

The whole process of the *yoga* system is to purify oneself. And what is this purification? Purification ensues upon the realization of one's actual identity. Purification is realizing that "I am pure spirit—I am not this matter." Due to material contact, we are identifying ourselves with matter, and we are thinking, "I am this body." But in order to perform real *yoga* one must realize his constitutional position as being distinct from matter. The purpose of seeking out a secluded place and executing the meditational process is to come to this understanding. It is not possible to come to this understanding if one executes the process improperly. In any case, this is the consideration of Lord Caitanya Mahāprabhu:

harer nāma harer nāma
harer nāmaiva kevalam
kalau nāsty eva nāsty eva
nāsty eva gatir anyathā

"In this age of quarrel and disagreement [Kali-yuga], there is no other way of spiritual realization but this chanting of the names. There is no other way, there is no other way, there is no other way."

It is generally thought, at least in the Western world, that the *yoga* system involves meditating on the void. But the Vedic literatures do not recommend meditating on any void. Rather, the *Vedas* maintain that *yoga* means meditation on Viṣṇu, and this is also maintained in *Bhagavad-gītā*. In many *yoga* societies we find that people sit cross-legged and very straight, then close their eyes to meditate, and so fifty percent of them go to sleep, because when we close our eyes and have no subject matter for contemplation, we simply go to sleep. Of course, this is not recommended by Śrī Kṛṣṇa in *Bhagavad-gītā*. One must sit very straight, and the eyes be only half-closed, gazing at the tip of one's nose. If one does not follow the instructions, the result will be sleep and nothing more. Sometimes, of course, meditation goes on when one is sleeping, but this is not the recommended process for the execution of *yoga*. Thus, to keep oneself awake Kṛṣṇa advises that one always keep the tip of the nose visible. In addition, one must be always undisturbed. If the mind is agitated or if there is a great deal of activity going on, one will not be able to concentrate. In meditational *yoga* one must also be devoid of fear. There is no question of fear when one enters spiritual life. And one must also be *brahmacārī*, completely free from sex life. Nor can there be any demands on one meditating in this way. When there are no demands, and one executes this system properly, then he can control his mind. After one has met all the requirements for meditation, he must transfer his whole thought to Kṛṣṇa, or Viṣṇu. It is not that one is to transfer his thought to vacancy. Thus Kṛṣṇa says that one absorbed in the meditational *yoga* system is "always thinking of Me."

The *yogī* obviously has to go through a great deal of difficulty to purify the *ātmā* (mind, body and soul), but it is a fact that this can be done most effectively in this age simply by the chanting of Hare Kṛṣṇa, Hare Kṛṣṇa, Kṛṣṇa Kṛṣṇa, Hare Hare/ Hare Rāma, Hare Rāma, Rāma Rāma, Hare Hare. Why is this? Because this transcendental sound vibration is nondifferent from Kṛṣṇa. When we chant His name with devotion, then Kṛṣṇa is with us, and when Kṛṣṇa is with us, then what is the possibility of remaining impure? Consequently, one absorbed in Kṛṣṇa consciousness, in chanting the names of Kṛṣṇa and serving Him always, receives the benefit of the highest form of *yoga*. The advantage is that he doesn't have to take all the trouble of the meditational process. That is the beauty of Kṛṣṇa consciousness.

In *yoga* it is necessary to control all of the senses, and when all the senses are controlled, the mind must be engaged in thinking of Viṣṇu. One becomes peaceful after thus conquering material life.

jitātmanaḥ praśāntasya
paramātmā samāhitaḥ

"For one who has conquered the mind, the Supersoul is already reached, for he has attained tranquillity." (Bg. 6.7) This material world has been likened to a great forest fire. As in the forest, fire may automatically take place, so in this material world, although we may try to live peacefully, there is always a great conflagration. It is not possible to live in peace anywhere in the material world. But for one who is transcendentally situated—either by the meditational *yoga* system or by the empirical philosophical method or by *bhakti-yoga*—peace is possible. All forms of *yoga* are meant for transcendental life, but the method of chanting is especially effective in this age. *Kīrtana* may go on for hours, and one may not feel tired, but it is difficult to sit in lotus position perfectly still for more than a few minutes. Yet regardless of the process, once the fire of material life is extinguished, one does not simply experience what is called impersonal void. Rather, as Kṛṣṇa tells Arjuna, one enters into the supreme abode.

yuñjann evaṁ sadātmānaṁ
yogī niyata-mānasaḥ
śāntiṁ nirvāṇa-paramāṁ
mat-saṁsthām adhigacchati

"By meditating in this manner, always controlling the body, mind and activities, the mystic transcendentalist attains to the kingdom of God through cessation of material existence." (Bg. 6.15) Kṛṣṇa's abode is not void. It is like an establishment, and in an establishment there is a variety of engagements. The successful *yogī* actually attains to the kingdom of God, where there is spiritual variegatedness.

The *yoga* processes are simply ways to elevate oneself to enter into that abode. Actually we belong to that abode, but being forgetful, we are put in this material world. Just as a madman becomes crazy and is put into a lunatic asylum, so we, losing sight of our spiritual identity, become crazy and are put into this material world. Thus the material world is a sort of lunatic asylum, and we can easily notice that nothing is done very sanely here. Our real business is to get out and enter into the kingdom of God. In *Bhagavad-gītā* Kṛṣṇa gives information of this kingdom and also gives instructions about His position and our position—of what He is and what we are. All the information necessary is set forth in *Bhagavad-gītā,* and a sane man will take advantage of this knowledge.

FOUR

Yoga as Body and Mind Control

THROUGHOUT *Bhagavad-gītā,* Kṛṣṇa was encouraging Arjuna to fight, for he was a warrior, and fighting was his duty. Although Kṛṣṇa delineates the meditational *yoga* system in the Sixth Chapter, He does not stress it or encourage Arjuna to pursue it as his path. Kṛṣṇa admits that this meditational process is very difficult:

śrī-bhaga vān uvāca
asaṁśayaṁ mahā-bāho
mano durnigrahaṁ calam
abhyāsena tu kaunteya
vairāgyeṇa ca gṛhyate

"The Blessed Lord said: O mighty-armed son of Kuntī, it is undoubtedly very difficult to curb the restless mind, but it is possible by constant practice and by detachment." (Bg. 6.35) Here Kṛṣṇa emphasizes practice and renunciation as ways to control the mind. But what is that renunciation? Today it is hardly possible for us to renounce anything, for we are so habituated to such a variety of material sense pleasures. Despite leading a life of uncontrolled sense indulgence, we attend *yoga* classes and expect to attain success. There are so many rules and regulations involved in the proper execution of *yoga,* and most of us can hardly give up a simple habit like smoking. In His discourse on the meditational *yoga* system, Kṛṣṇa proclaims that *yoga* cannot bc propcrly performed by one who eats too much or eats too little. One who starves himself cannot properly perform *yoga.* Nor can the person who eats more than required. The eating process should be moderate, just enough to keep body and soul together; it should not be for the enjoyment of the tongue. When palatable dishes come before us, we are accustomed to take not just one of the preparations but two, three and four—and upwards. Our tongue is never satisfied. But it is not unusual in India to see a *yogī* take only a small spoonful of rice a day and nothing more. Nor can one execute the meditational *yoga* system if one sleeps too much or does not sleep sufficiently. Kṛṣṇa does not say that there is such a thing as dreamless sleep. As soon as we go to sleep, we will have a dream, although we may not remember it. In the *Gītā* Kṛṣṇa cautions that one who dreams too much while sleeping cannot properly execute *yoga.* One should not sleep more than six hours daily. Nor can one infected by insomnia, who cannot sleep at night, successfully execute *yoga,* for the body must be kept fit. Thus Kṛṣṇa outlines so many requirements for disciplining the body. All these requirements, however, can essentially be broken down into four basic rules: no illicit sexual connection, no intoxication, no meat-eating and no gambling. These are the four minimum regulations for the execution of any *yoga* system. And in this age who can refrain from these activities? We have to test ourselves accordingly to ascertain our success in *yoga* execution.

yogī yuñjīta satatam
ātmānaṁ rahasi sthitaḥ
ekākī yata-cittātmā
nirāśīr aparigrahaḥ

"A transcendentalist should always try to concentrate his mind on the Supreme Self; he should live alone in a secluded place and should always carefully control his mind. He should be free from desires and feelings of possessiveness." (Bg. 6.10) From this verse we can understand that it is the duty of the *yogī* to always remain alone. Meditational *yoga* cannot be performed in an assembly, at least not according to *Bhagavad-gītā.* In the meditational system it is not possible to concentrate the mind upon the Supersoul except in a secluded place. In India, there are still many *yogīs* who assemble at the Kumba Melā. Generally they are in seclusion, but on rare occasions they come to attend special functions. In India there are still thousands of *yogīs* and sages, and every twelve years or so they meet in particular holy places—Allahabad, etc.—just as in America they have businessmen's conventions. The *yogī,* in addition to living in a secluded place, should also be free from desires and should not think that he is performing *yoga* to achieve some material powers. Nor should he accept gifts or favours from people. If he is properly executing this meditational *yoga,* he stays alone in the jungles, forests or mountains and avoids society altogether. At all times he must be convinced for whom he has become a *yogī*. He does not consider himself alone because at all times the Paramātmā—Supersoul—is with him. From this we can see that in modern civilization it is indeed very difficult to execute this meditational form of *yoga* properly. Contemporary civilization in this age of Kali has actually made it impossible for us to be alone, to be desireless and to be possessionless.

The method of executing meditational *yoga* is further explained in considerable detail by Kṛṣṇa to Arjuna. Śrī Kṛṣṇa says,

śucau deśe pratiṣṭhāpya
sthiram āsanam ātmanaḥ
nāty-ucchritaṁ nāti-nīcaṁ
cailājina-kuśottaram

tatraikāgraṁ manaḥ kṛtvā
yata-cittendriya-kriyaḥ
upaviśyāsane yuñjyād
yogam ātma-viśuddhaye

"To practice *yoga*, one should go to a secluded place and should lay *kuśa* grass on the ground and then cover it with a deerskin and a soft cloth. The seat should be neither too high nor too low and should be situated in a sacred place. The *yogī* should then sit on it very firmly and should practice *yoga* by controlling the mind and the senses, purifying the heart and fixing the mind on one point." (Bg. 6.11–12) Generally *yogīs* sit on tigerskin or deerskin because reptiles will not crawl on such skins to disturb their meditations. It seems that in God's creation there is a use for everything. Every grass and herb has its use and serves some function, although we may not know what it is. So in *Bhagavad-gītā* Kṛṣṇa has made some provision whereby the *yogī* doesn't have to worry about snakes. Having acquired a good sitting place in a secluded environment, the *yogī* begins to purify the *ātmā*—body, mind and soul. The *yogī* should not think, "Now I will try to achieve some wonderful powers." Sometimes *yogīs* do attain certain *siddhis,* or powers, but these are not the purpose of *yoga,* and real *yogīs* do not exhibit them. The real *yogī* thinks, "I am now contaminated by this material atmosphere, so now I must purify myself."

We can quickly see that controlling the mind and body is not such an easy thing and that we cannot control them as easily as we can go to the store and purchase something. But Kṛṣṇa indicates that these rules can be easily followed when we are in Kṛṣṇa consciousness.

Of course everyone is motivated by sex life, but sex life is not actually discouraged. We have this material body, and as long as we have it, sex desire will be there. Similarly, as long as we have the body, we must eat to maintain it, and we must sleep in order to give it rest. We cannot expect to negate these activities, but the Vedic literatures do give us guidelines for regulation in eating, sleeping, mating, etc. If we at all expect success in the *yoga* system, we cannot allow our unbridled senses to take us down the paths of sense objects; therefore guidelines are set up. Lord Śrī Kṛṣṇa is advising that the mind can be controlled through regulation. If we do not regulate our activities, our mind will be more and more agitated. It is not that activities are to be stopped, but regulated by the mind always engaged in Kṛṣṇa consciousness. Being always engaged in some activity connected with Kṛṣṇa is actual *samādhi.* It is not that when one is in *samādhi* he doesn't eat, work, sleep or enjoy himself in any way. Rather, *samādhi* can be defined as executing regulated activities while absorbed in the thought of Kṛṣṇa.

asaṁyatātmanā yogo
duṣprāpa iti me matiḥ
vaśyātmanā tu yatatā
śakyo 'vāptum upāyataḥ

"For one whose mind is unbridled," Kṛṣṇa further says, "self-realization is difficult work." (Bg. 6.36) Anyone knows that an unbridled horse is dangerous to ride. He can go in any direction at any speed, and his rider is likely to come to some harm. Insofar as the mind is unbridled, Kṛṣṇa agrees with Arjuna that the *yoga* system is very difficult work indeed. "But," Kṛṣṇa adds, "he whose mind is controlled and strives by right means is assured of success. That is My judgement." (Bg. 6.36) What is meant by "strives by right means"? One has to try to follow the four basic regulative principles as mentioned and execute his activities absorbed in Kṛṣṇa consciousness.

If one wants to engage in *yoga* at home, then he has to make certain that his other engagements are moderate. He cannot spend long hours of the day working hard to simply earn a livelihood. One should work very moderately, eat very moderately, gratify the senses very moderately and keep his life as free from anxiety as possible. In this way practice of *yoga* may be successful.

What is the sign by which we can tell that one has attained perfection in *yoga*? Kṛṣṇa indicates that one is situated in *yoga* when his consciousness is completely under his control.

yadā viniyataṁ cittam
ātmany evāvatiṣṭhate
nispṛhaḥ sarva-kāmebhyo
yukta ity ucyate tadā

"When the *yogī,* by practice of *yoga,* disciplines his mental activities and becomes situated in Transcendence—devoid of all material desires—he is said to have attained *yoga.*" (Bg. 6.18) One who has attained *yoga* is not dependent on the dictations of his mind; rather, the mind comes under his control. Nor is the mind put out or extinguished, for it is the business of the *yogī* to think of Kṛṣṇa, or Viṣṇu, always. The *yogī* cannot allow his mind to go out. This may sound very difficult, but it is possible in Kṛṣṇa consciousness. When one is always engaged in Kṛṣṇa consciousness, in the service of Kṛṣṇa, then how is it possible for the mind to wander away from Kṛṣṇa? In the service of Kṛṣṇa, the mind is automatically controlled.

Nor should the *yogī* have any desire for material sense gratification. If one is in Kṛṣṇa consciousness, he has no desire other than Kṛṣṇa. It is not possible to become desireless. The desire for sense gratification must be overcome by the process of purification, but desire for Kṛṣṇa should be cultivated. It is simply that we have to transfer the desire. There is no question of killing desire, for desire is the constant companion of the living entity. Kṛṣṇa consciousness is the process by which one purifies his desires; instead of desiring so many things for sense gratification, one simply desires things for the service of Kṛṣṇa. For example, we may desire palatable food, but instead of preparing foodstuffs for ourselves, we can prepare them for Kṛṣṇa and offer them to Him. It is not that the action is different, but there is a transfer of consciousness from thinking of acting for my senses to thinking of acting for Kṛṣṇa. We may prepare nice milk products, vegetables, grains, fruits and other vegetarian dishes for Kṛṣṇa and then offer them to Him, praying, "This material body is a lump of ignorance and the senses are a network of paths leading to death. Of all the senses the tongue is the most voracious and difficult to control. It is very difficult to conquer the tongue in this world; therefore Śrī Kṛṣṇa has given us this nice *prasāda,* spiritual food, to conquer the tongue. So let us take this *prasāda* to our full satisfaction and glorify Their Lordships Śrī Śrī Rādhā and Kṛṣṇa and in love call for the help of Lord Caitanya and Nityānanda Prabhu." In this way our *karma* is sacrificed, for from the very beginning we are thinking that the food is being offered to Kṛṣṇa. We should have no personal desires for the food. Kṛṣṇa is so merciful, however, that he gives us the food to eat. In this way our desire is fulfilled. When one has moulded his life in such a way—dovetailing his desires to Kṛṣṇa's—then it is to be understood that he has attained perfection in *yoga.* Simply breathing deeply and doing some exercises is not *yoga* as far as *Bhagavad-gītā* is concerned. A whole purification of consciousness is required.

In the execution of *yoga,* it is very important that the mind is not agitated.

yathā dīpo nivāta-stho
neṅgate sopamā smṛtā
yogino yata-cittasya
yuñjato yogam ātmanaḥ

"As a lamp in a windless place does not waver, so the transcendentalist, whose mind is controlled, remains always steady in his meditation on the transcendent self." (Bg. 6.19) When a candle is in a windless place, its flame remains straight and does not waver. The mind, like the flame, is susceptible to so many material desires that with the slightest agitation it will move. A little movement of the mind can change the whole consciousness. Therefore in India one seriously practicing *yoga* traditionally remained *brahmacārī*, or celibate.

There are two kinds of *brahmacārī:* one is completely celibate and the other is *gṛhastha-brahmacārī*, that is to say he has a wife, he does not associate with any other woman, and his relations with his own wife are strictly regulated. In this way, either by complete celibacy or restricted sex life, one's mind is kept from being agitated. Yet when one takes a vow to remain a complete celibate, his mind may still be agitated by sexual desire; therefore in India those practicing the traditional *yoga* under strict vows of celibacy are not allowed to sit alone even with a mother, sister or daughter. The mind is so fickle that the slightest suggestion can create havoc.

The *yogī* should have his mind trained in such a way that as soon as his mind wanders from meditation on Viṣṇu, he drags it back again. This requires a great deal of practice. One must come to know that his real happiness is in experiencing the pleasure of his transcendental senses, not the material senses. Senses are not to be sacrificed, and desires are not to be sacrificed, but there are both desires and sense satisfaction in the spiritual sphere. Real happiness is transcendental to material, sensual experience. If one is not convinced of this, he will surely be agitated and will fall down. One should therefore know that the happiness he is trying to derive from material senses is not really happiness.

Those who are actually *yogīs* truly enjoy, but how do they enjoy? *Ramante yogino 'nante*—their enjoyment is unlimited, that unlimited enjoyment is real happiness, and such happiness is spiritual, not material. This is the real meaning of *Rāma,* as in the chant Hare Rāma. *Rāma* means enjoyment through spiritual life. Spiritual life is all pleasure, and Kṛṣṇa is all pleasure. We do not have to sacrifice pleasure, but we do have to enjoy it properly. A diseased man cannot enjoy life; his enjoyment of life is a false enjoyment. But when he is cured and is healthy, then he is able to enjoy. Similarly, as long as we are in the material conception of life, we are not actually enjoying ourselves but are simply becoming more and more entangled in material nature. If a sick man is not supposed to eat, his eating unrestrictedly actually kills him. Similarly, the more we increase material enjoyment, the more we become entangled in this world, and the more difficult it becomes to get free from the material entrapment. All of the systems of *yoga* are meant to disentangle the conditioned soul from this entrapment, to transfer him from the false enjoyment of material things to the actual enjoyment of Kṛṣṇa consciousness. Śrī Kṛṣṇa says,

yatroparamate cittaṁ
niruddhaṁ yoga-sevayā
yatra caivātmanātmānaṁ
paśyann ātmani tuṣyati

sukham ātyantikaṁ yat tad
buddhi-grāhyam atīndriyam

His Divine Grace
A.C. Bhaktivedanta Swami Prabhupāda
Founder-*Ācārya* of the International Society for Krishna Consciousness

After hearing Lord Kṛṣṇa speak the *Bhagavad-gītā*, Arjuna set aside his misgivings and fought. (p. 2)

Thinking of Kṛṣṇa is the essence of all *yoga* systems. (p. 9)

Kṛṣṇa's abode is not void—it is like an establishment where there are a variety of engagements. (p. 15)

The Supersoul is always seated within the heart along with the individual soul. (p. 31)

Bhagavān Śrī Kṛṣṇa is full of all opulence as the Supreme Personality of Godhead. (p. 47)

We can love the Supreme Lord as master, as friend, as child or as husband. (p. 50)

Kṛṣṇa consciousness is the last link in the yogic chain, the link that binds us to the Supreme Person, Lord Śrī Kṛṣṇa. (p. 56)

vetti yatra na caivāyaṁ
sthitaś calati tattvataḥ

yaṁ labdhvā cāparaṁ lābhaṁ
manyate nādhikaṁ tataḥ
yasmin sthito na duḥkhena
guruṇāpi vicālyate

taṁ vidyād duḥkha-saṁyoga-
viyogaṁ yoga-saṁjñitam

"In the stage of perfection called trance, or *samādhi*, one's mind is completely restrained from material mental activities by practice of *yoga*. This is characterized by one's ability to see the self by the pure mind and to relish and rejoice in the self. In that joyous state, one is situated in boundless transcendental happiness and enjoys himself through transcendental senses. Established thus, one never departs from the truth, and upon gaining this he thinks there is no greater gain. Being situated in such a position, one is never shaken, even in the midst of greatest difficulty. This indeed is actual freedom from all miseries arising from material contact." (Bg. 6.20–23)

One form of *yoga* may be difficult and another may be easy, but in all cases one must purify his existence to the conception of Kṛṣṇa conscious enjoyment. Then one will be happy.

yadā hi nendriyārtheṣu
na karmasv anuṣajjate
sarva-saṅkalpa-sannyāsī
yogārūḍhas tadocyate

uddhared ātmanātmānaṁ
nātmānam avasādayet
ātmaiva hy ātmano bandhur
ātmaiva ripur ātmanaḥ

"A person is said to have attained to *yoga* when, having renounced all material desires, he neither acts for sense gratification nor engages in fruitive activities. A man must elevate himself by his own mind, not degrade himself. The mind is the friend of the conditioned soul, and his enemy as well." (Bg. 6.4–5) We have to raise ourselves to the spiritual standard by ourselves. In this sense I am my own friend and I am my own enemy. The opportunity is ours. There is a very nice verse by Cāṇakya Paṇḍita: "No one is anyone's friend, no one is anyone's enemy. It is only by behavior that one can understand who is his friend and who is his enemy." No one is born our enemy, and no one is born our friend. These roles are determined by mutual behavior. As we have dealings with others in ordinary affairs, in the same way the individual has dealings with himself. I may act as my own friend or as an enemy. As a friend, I can understand my position as spirit soul and, seeing that somehow or other I have come into contact with material nature, try to get free from material entanglement by acting in such a way as to disentangle myself. In this case I am my friend. But if even after getting this opportunity I do not take it, then I should be considered my own worst enemy.

bandhur ātmātmanas tasya
yenātmaivātmanā jitaḥ
anātmanas tu śatrutve
vartetātmaiva śatru-vat

"For he who has conquered the mind, the mind is the best of friends; but for one who has failed to do so, his very mind will be the greatest enemy." (Bg. 6.6) How is it possible for one to become his own friend? This is explained here. *Ātmā* means "mind," "body" and "soul." When we speak of *ātmā,* insofar as we are in the bodily conception, we refer to the body. However, when we transcend the bodily conception and rise to the mental platform, *ātmā* refers to the mind. But actually when we are situated on the truly spiritual platform, then *ātmā* refers to the soul. In actuality we are pure spirit. In this way, according to one's spiritual development, the meaning of the word *ātmā* differs. As far as the *Nirukti* Vedic dictionary is concerned, *ātmā* refers to body, mind and soul. However, in this verse of *Bhagavad-gītā, ātmā* refers to mind.

If, through *yoga,* the mind can be trained, then the mind is our friend. But if the mind is left untrained, then there is no possibility of leading a successful life. For one who has no idea of spiritual life, the mind is the enemy. If one thinks that he is simply the body, his mind will not be working for his benefit; it will simply be acting to serve the gross body and to further condition the living entity and entrap him in material nature. If, however, one understands one's position as spirit soul apart from the body, the mind can be a liberating factor. In itself, the mind has nothing to do; it is simply waiting to be trained, and it is best trained through association. Desire is the function of the mind, and one desires according to his association; so if the mind is to act as friend, there must be good association.

The best association is a *sādhu,* that is, a Kṛṣṇa conscious person or one who is striving for spiritual realization. There are those who are striving for temporary things (*asat*).

Matter and the body are temporary, and if one only engages himself for bodily pleasure, he is conditioned by temporary things. But if he engages himself in self-realization, then he is engaged in something permanent (*sat*). Obviously if one is intelligent he will associate with those who are trying to elevate themselves to the platform of self-realization through one of the various forms of *yoga*. The result will be that those who are *sādhu*, or realized, will be able to sever his attachment to material association. This is the great advantage of good association. For instance, Kṛṣṇa speaks *Bhagavad-gītā* to Arjuna just to cut off his attachment to this material affection. Because Arjuna is attracted to things that are impeding the execution of his own duty, Kṛṣṇa severs these things. To cut something, a sharp instrument is required; and to cut the mind from its attachments, sharp words are often required. The *sādhu* or teacher shows no mercy in using sharp words to sever the student's mind from material attractions. By speaking the truth uncompromisingly, he is able to sever the bondage. For example, at the very beginning of *Bhagavad-gītā* Kṛṣṇa speaks sharply to Arjuna by telling him that although he speaks like a learned man, he is actually fool number one. If we actually want detachment from this material world, we should be prepared to accept such cutting words from the spiritual master. Compromise and flattery have no effect where strong words are required.

In *Bhagavad-gītā* the material conception of life is condemned in so many places. One who thinks the country in which he is born is worshipable, or one who goes to holy places and yet ignores the *sādhus* there, is likened unto an ass. As an enemy is always thinking of doing harm, so the untrained mind will drag one deeper and deeper into material entanglement. Conditioned souls struggle very hard with the mind and with the other senses. Since the mind directs the other senses, it is of utmost importance to make the mind the friend.

jitātmanaḥ praśāntasya
paramātmā samāhitaḥ
śītoṣṇa-sukha-duḥkheṣu
tathā mānāpamānayoḥ

"For one who has conquered the mind, the Supersoul is already reached, for he has attained tranquillity. To such a man happiness and distress, heat and cold, honour and dishonour are all the same." (Bg. 6.7) By training the mind, one actually attains tranquillity, for the mind is always dragging us over nonpermanent things, just as an unbridled horse will pull a chariot on a perilous course. Although we are permanent and eternal, somehow or other we have become attracted to nonpermanent things. But the mind can be easily trained if it is simply fixed on Kṛṣṇa. Just as a fort is safe when it is defended by a great general, if Kṛṣṇa is placed in the fort of the mind, there will be no possibility of the enemy's entering. Material education, wealth and power will not help one to control the mind. A great devotee prays, "When will I be able to think of You constantly? My mind is always dragging me about, but as soon as I am able to fix my mind on the lotus feet of Kṛṣṇa, it becomes clear." When the mind is clear, it is possible to meditate on the Supersoul. The Paramātmā, or Supersoul, is always seated within the heart along with the individual soul. The *yoga* system involves concentrating the mind and focusing it on the Paramātmā, or Supersoul, seated within the heart. The previously quoted verse from *Bhagavad-gītā* indicates that one who has conquered the mind and has overcome all attachment to nonpermanent things can be absorbed in thought of the Paramātmā. One so absorbed becomes free from all duality and false designations.

FIVE

Yoga as Freedom from Duality and Designation

THIS MATERIAL WORLD is a world of duality—at one moment we are subjected to the heat of the summer season and at the next moment the cold of winter. Or at one moment we're happy and at the next moment distressed. At one moment honoured, at the next dishonoured. In the material world of duality, it is impossible to understand one thing without understanding its opposite. It is not possible to understand what honour is unless I understand dishonour. Similarly, I cannot understand what misery is if I have never tasted happiness. Nor can I understand what happiness is unless I have tasted misery. One has to transcend such dualities, but as long as this body is here these dualities will be here also. Insofar as one strives to get out of bodily conceptions—not out of the body but out of bodily conceptions—one has to learn to tolerate such dualities. In the Second Chapter of *Bhagavad-gītā* Kṛṣṇa informs Arjuna that the duality of distress and happiness is due to the body alone. It's like a skin disease, or skin itch. Just because there is itching, one should not be mad after it to scratch it. We should not go mad or give up our duty just because mosquitoes bite us. There are so many dualities one has to tolerate, but if the mind is fixed in Kṛṣṇa consciousness, all these dualities will seem insignificant.

How is it one can tolerate such dualities?

jñāna-vijñāna-tṛptātmā
kūṭa-stho vijitendriyaḥ
yukta ity ucyate yogī
sama-loṣṭrāśma-kāñcanaḥ

"A person is said to be established in self-realization and is called a *yogī* (or mystic) when he is fully satisfied by virtue of acquired knowledge and realization. Such a person is situated in transcendence and is self-controlled. He sees everything—whether it be pebbles, stones or gold—as the same." (Bg. 6.8) *Jñāna* means theoretical knowledge, and *vijñāna* refers to practical knowledge. For instance, a science student has to study theoretical scientific conceptions as well as applied science. Theoretical knowledge alone will not help. One has to be able to also apply this knowledge. Similarly, in *yoga* one should have not only theoretical knowledge but practical knowledge. Simply understanding "I am not this body" and at the same time acting in a nonsensical way will not help. There are so many societies where the members seriously discuss Vedānta philosophy while smoking and drinking and enjoying a sensual life. It will not help if one only has knowledge theoretically. This knowledge must be demonstrated. One who truly understands "I am not this body" will actually reduce his bodily necessities to a minimum. When one increases the demands of the body while thinking "I am not this body," then of what use is that knowledge? A person can only be satisfied when there is *jñāna* and *vijñāna* side by side.

When a person is situated on the practical level of spiritual realization, it should be understood he is actually situated in *yoga*. It is not that one should continue to attend *yoga* classes and yet remain the same throughout his life; there must be practical realization. And what is the sign of that practical realization? The mind will be calm and quiet and no longer agitated by the attraction of the material world. Thus self-controlled, one is not attracted by the material glitter, and he sees everything—pebbles, stones or gold—as the same. In the material civilization, so much paraphernalia is produced just to satisfy the senses. These things are produced under the banner of material advancement. He who is situated in *yoga* sees such paraphernalia as just so much rubbish in the street. Moreover,

suhṛn-mitrāry-udāsīna-
madhyastha-dveṣya-bandhuṣu
sādhuṣv api ca pāpeṣu
sama-buddhir viśiṣyate

"A person is said to be still further advanced when he regards all—the honest well-wisher, friends and enemies, the envious, the pious, the sinner and those who are indifferent and impartial—with an equal mind." (Bg. 6.9) There are different kinds of friends. There is *suhṛt*, who is by nature a well-wisher and is always desiring one's welfare. *Mitra* refers to an ordinary friend, and *udāsīna* is one who is neutral. In this material world someone may be my well-wisher, friend or neither friend nor enemy but neutral. Someone else may serve as a mediator between me and my enemies, and in this verse he is called *madhya-stha.* One may also see someone as pious and another as sinful according to his own calculations. But when he is situated in transcendence, all of these—friends, enemies or whatever—cease to exist. When one becomes actually learned, he does not see any enemy or any friend because in actuality "no one is my enemy, no one is my friend, no one is my father, no one is my mother, etc." We are all simply living entities playing on a stage in the dress of father, mother, children, friend, enemy, sinner and saint, etc. It is like a great drama with so many characters playing their parts. However, on the stage a person may be an enemy or whatever, but off the stage all the actors are friends. Similarly, with these bodies we are playing on the stage of material nature, and we attach so many designations to one another. I may be thinking, "This is my son," but in actuality I cannot beget any son. It is not possible. At the utmost I can only beget a body. It is not within any man's power to beget a living entity. Merely by sexual intercourse a living entity cannot be begotten. The living entity must be *placed* in the emulsification of secretions. This is the verdict of *Śrīmad-Bhāgavatam.* Thus all the multifarious relationships between bodies are just so much stage play. One who is actually realized and has actually attained *yoga* no longer sees these bodily distinctions.

SIX

The Fate of the Unsuccessful Yogī

IT IS NOT that *Bhagavad-gītā* rejects the meditational *yoga* process; it recognizes it as a bona fide method, but it further indicates that it is not possible in this age. Thus the subject in the Sixth Chapter of *Bhagavad-gītā* is quickly dropped by Śrī Kṛṣṇa and Arjuna. Arjuna next asks,

ayatiḥ śraddhayopeto
yogāc calita-mānasaḥ
aprāpya yoga-saṁsiddhiṁ
kāṁ gatiṁ kṛṣṇa gacchati

"What is the destination of the man of faith who does not persevere, who in the beginning takes to the process of self-realization but who later desists due to worldly-mindedness and thus does not attain perfection in mysticism?" (Bg. 6.37) In other words, he is asking what becomes of the unsuccessful *yogī,* or the person who attempts to perform *yoga* but somehow desists and does not succeed. It is something like a student who does not get his degree because he drops out of school. Elsewhere in the *Gītā*, Śrī Kṛṣṇa points out to Arjuna that out of many men, few strive for perfection, and out of those who strive for perfection, only a few succeed. So Arjuna is inquiring after the vast number of failures. Even if a man has faith and strives for perfection in the *yoga* system, Arjuna points out that he may not attain this perfection due to "worldly-mindedness."

kaccin nobhaya-vibhraṣṭaś
chinnābhram iva naśyati
apratiṣṭho mahā-bāho
vimūḍho brahmaṇaḥ pathi

"O mighty-armed Kṛṣṇa," Arjuna continues, "does not such a man, being deviated from the path of Transcendence, perish like a riven cloud, with no position in any sphere?" (Bg. 6.38) When a cloud is torn apart by the wind, it does not mend back together again.

etan me saṁśayaṁ kṛṣṇa
chettum arhasy aśeṣataḥ
tvad-anyaḥ saṁśayasyāsya
chettā na hy upapadyate

"This is my doubt, O Kṛṣṇa, and I ask You to dispel it completely. But for Yourself, no one is to be found who can destroy this doubt." (Bg. 6.39) Arjuna is asking this question about the fate of the unsuccessful *yogī* so that in the future people would not be discouraged. By a *yogī*, Arjuna is referring to the *haṭha-yogī, jñāna-yogī* and *bhakti-yogī;* it is not that meditation is the only form of *yoga*. The meditator, the philosopher and the devotee are all to be considered *yogīs*. Arjuna is questioning for all those who are attempting to become successful transcendentalists. And how does Śrī Kṛṣṇa answer him?

śrī-bhagavān uvāca
pārtha naiveha nāmutra
vināśas tasya vidyate
na hi kalyāṇa-kṛt kaścid
durgatiṁ tāta gacchati

Here, as in many other places throughout the *Gītā*, Śrī Kṛṣṇa is referred to as Bhagavān. This is another of the Lord's innumerable names. *Bhagavān* indicates that Kṛṣṇa is the proprietor of six opulences: He possesses all beauty, all wealth, all power, all fame, all knowledge and all renunciation. Living entities partake of these opulences in finite degrees. One may be famous in a family, in a town, in a country or on one planet, but no one is famous throughout the creation, as is Śrī Kṛṣṇa. The leaders of the world may be famous for a few years only, but Lord Śrī Kṛṣṇa appeared five thousand years ago and is still being worshipped. So one who possesses all six of these opulences in completeness is considered to be God. In *Bhagavad-gītā* Kṛṣṇa speaks to Arjuna as the Supreme Personality of Godhead, and as such it is to be understood that He has complete knowledge. *Bhagavad-gītā* was imparted to the sun-god and to Arjuna by Kṛṣṇa, but nowhere is it mentioned that *Bhagavad-gītā* was imparted to Kṛṣṇa. Why? Complete knowledge means that He knows everything that is to be known. This is an attribute of God alone. Being that Kṛṣṇa knows everything, Arjuna is putting this question to Him about the fate of the unsuccessful *yogī*. There is no possibility for Arjuna to research the truth. He simply has to receive the truth from the complete source, and this is the system of disciplic succession. Kṛṣṇa is complete, and the knowledge that comes from Kṛṣṇa is also complete. If Arjuna receives this complete knowledge and we receive it from Arjuna as it was spoken to him, then we also receive complete knowledge. And what is this knowledge? "The Blessed Lord said: Son of Pṛthā, a transcendentalist engaged in auspicious activities does not meet with destruction either in this world or in the spiritual world; one who does good, My friend, is never overcome by evil." (Bg. 6.40) Here Kṛṣṇa indicates that the very striving for *yoga* perfection is a most auspicious attempt. When one attempts something so auspicious, he is never degraded.

Actually Arjuna is asking a very appropriate and intelligent question. It is not unusual for one to fall down from the platform of devotional service. Sometimes a neophyte devotee does not keep the rules and regulations. Sometimes he yields to intoxication or is trapped by some feminine attractions. These are impediments on the path of *yoga* perfection. But Śrī Kṛṣṇa gives an encouraging answer, for He tells Arjuna that even if one sincerely cultivates only one-percent worth of spiritual knowledge, he will never fall down into the material whirlpool. That is due to the sincerity of his effort. It should always be understood that we are weak and that the material energy is very strong. To adopt spiritual life is more or less to declare war against the material energy. The material energy is trying to entrap the conditioned soul as much as possible, and when the conditioned soul tries to get out of her clutches by spiritual advancement of knowledge, material nature becomes more stringent and vigorous in her efforts to test how much the aspiring spiritualist is sincere. The material energy, or *māyā,* will then offer more allurements.

In this regard, there is the story of Viśvāmitra Muni, a great king, a *kṣatriya,* who renounced his kingdom and took to the *yoga* process in order to become more spiritually advanced. At that time the meditational *yoga* process was possible to execute. Viśvāmitra Muni meditated so intently that Indra, the King of heaven, noticed him and thought, "This man is trying to occupy my post." The heavenly planets are also material, and there is competition—no businessman wants another businessman to exceed him. Fearing that Viśvāmitra Muni would actually depose him, Indra sent one heavenly society girl, named Menakā, to allure him sexually. Menakā was naturally very beautiful, and she was intent on disrupting the *muni's* meditations. Indeed, he became aware of her feminine presence upon hearing the sound of her bangles, and he immediately looked up from his meditation, saw her, and became captivated by her beauty. As a result, the beautiful girl Śakuntalā was born by their conjugation. When Śakuntalā was born, Viśvāmitra lamented: "Oh, I was just trying to cultivate spiritual knowledge, and again I have been entrapped." He was about to flee when Menakā brought his beautiful daughter before him and chastised him. Despite her pleading, Viśvāmitra resolved to leave anyway.

Thus there is every chance of failure on the yogic path; even a great sage like Viśvāmitra Muni can fall down due to material allurement. Although the *muni* fell for the time being, he again resolved to go on with the *yoga* process, and this should be our resolve. Kṛṣṇa informs us that such failures should not be cause for despair. There is the famous proverb that "failure is the pillar of success." In the spiritual life especially, failure is not discouraging. Kṛṣṇa very clearly states that even if there is failure, there is no loss either in this world or in the next. One who takes to this auspicious line of spiritual culture is never completely vanquished.

Now what actually happens to the unsuccessful spiritualist? Śrī Kṛṣṇa specifically explains,

prāpya puṇya-kṛtāṁ lokān
uṣitvā śāśvatīḥ samāḥ
śucīnāṁ śrīmatāṁ gehe
yoga-bhraṣṭo 'bhijāyate

athavā yoginām eva
kule bhavati dhīmatām
etad dhi durlabhataraṁ
loke janma yad īdṛśam

"The unsuccessful *yogī*, after many, many years of enjoyment on the planets of the pious living entities, is born into a family of righteous people, or into a family of rich aristocracy. Or he takes his birth in a family of transcendentalists who are surely great in wisdom. Verily, such a birth is rare in this world." (Bg. 6.41–42) There are many planets in the universe, and on the higher planets there are greater comforts, the duration of life is longer, and the inhabitants are more religious and godly. Since it is said that six months on earth is equal to one day on the higher planets, the unsuccessful *yogī* stays on these higher planets for many, many years. Vedic literatures describe their lifetimes as lasting ten thousand years. So even if one is a failure, he is promoted to these higher planets. But one cannot remain there perpetually. When the fruits or the results of one's pious activities expire, he has to return to earth. Yet even upon returning to this planet, the unsuccessful *yogī* meets with fortunate circumstances, for he takes his birth in either a very rich family or a pious one.

Generally, according to the law of *karma,* if one enacts pious deeds, he is rewarded in the next life by birth into a very aristocratic family or into a very wealthy family, or he becomes a great scholar, or he is born very beautiful. In any case, those who sincerely begin spiritual life are guaranteed human birth in the next life—not only human birth, but birth into either a very pious or a very wealthy family. Thus one with such a good birth should understand that his fortune is due to his previous pious activities and to God's grace. These facilities are given by the Lord, who is always willing to give us the means to attain Him. Kṛṣṇa simply wants to see that we are sincere. In the *Śrīmad-Bhāgavatam* it is stated that every particular person has his own duty in life, regardless of his position and regardless of his society. If, however, he gives up his prescribed duty and somehow—either out of sentiment or association or craziness or whatever—takes shelter of Kṛṣṇa, and if, due to his immaturity, he falls from the devotional path, still there is no loss for him. On the other hand, if a person executes his duties perfectly but does not approach God, then what does he earn? His life is indeed without benefit. But a person who has approached Kṛṣṇa is better situated, even though he may fall down from the yogic platform.

Kṛṣṇa further indicates that of all good families to be born into—families of successful merchants or philosophers or meditators—the best is the family of *yogīs*. One who takes birth in a very rich family may be misled. It is normal for a man who is given great riches to try to enjoy those riches; thus rich men's sons often become drunkards or prostitute hunters. Similarly, one who takes birth in a pious family or in a brahminical family often becomes very puffed up and proud, thinking, "I am a *brāhmaṇa;* I am a pious man." There is chance of degradation in both rich and pious families, but one who takes birth in a family of *yogīs* or of devotees has a much better chance of cultivating again that spiritual life from which he has fallen. Kṛṣṇa tells Arjuna,

tatra taṁ buddhi-saṁyogaṁ
labhate paurva-dehikam
yatate ca tato bhūyaḥ
saṁsiddhau kuru-nandana

"On taking such a birth, he again revives the divine consciousness of his previous life, and he tries to make further progress in order to achieve complete success, O son of Kuru." (Bg. 6.43)

Being born in a family of those who execute *yoga* or devotional service, one remembers his spiritual activities executed in his previous life. Anyone who takes to Kṛṣṇa consciousness seriously is not an ordinary person; he must have taken to the same process in his previous life. Why is this?

pūrvābhyāsena tenaiva
hriyate hy avaśo 'pi saḥ

"By virtue of the divine consciousness of his previous life, he automatically becomes attracted to the yogic principles—even without seeking them." (Bg. 6.44) In the material world, we have experience that we do not carry our assets from one life to another. I may have millions of dollars in the bank, but as soon as my body is finished, my bank balance is also. At death, the bank balance does not go with me; it remains in the bank to be enjoyed by somebody else. This is not the case with spiritual culture. Even if one enacts a very small amount on the spiritual platform, he takes that with him to his next life, and he picks up again from that point.

When one picks up this knowledge that was interrupted, he should know that he should now finish the balance and complete the yogic process. One should not take the chance of finishing up the process in another birth but should resolve to finish it in this life. We should be determined in this way: "Somehow or other in my last life, I did not finish my spiritual cultivation. Now Kṛṣṇa has given me another opportunity, so let me finish it up in this life." Thus after leaving this body one will not again take birth in this material world, where birth, old age, disease and death are omnipresent, but will return to Kṛṣṇa. One who takes shelter under the lotus feet of Kṛṣṇa sees this material world simply as a place of danger. For one who takes to spiritual culture, this material world is actually unfit. Śrīla Bhaktisiddhānta Sarasvatī used to say, "This place is not fit for a gentleman." Once one has approached Kṛṣṇa and has attempted to make spiritual progress, Kṛṣṇa, who is situated within the heart, begins to give directions. In the *Gītā*, Śrī Kṛṣṇa says that for one who wants to remember Him, He gives remembrance, and for one who wants to forget Him, He allows him to forget.

SEVEN

Yoga as Reestablishing Relations with Kṛṣṇa

WE HAVE HEARD many times of the *yoga* system. The *yoga* system is approved by *Bhagavad-gītā,* but the *yoga* system in *Bhagavad-gītā* is especially meant for purification. The aim is threefold: to control the senses, to purify activities and to link oneself to Kṛṣṇa in a reciprocal relationship.

The Absolute Truth is realized in three stages: impersonal Brahman, localized Paramātmā (Supersoul) and ultimately Bhagavān, the Supreme Personality of Godhead. In the final analysis, the Supreme Absolute Truth is a person. Simultaneously He is the all-pervading Supersoul within the hearts of all living entities and within the core of all atoms, and He is the *brahmajyoti,* or the effulgence of spiritual light, as well. Bhagavān Śrī Kṛṣṇa is full of all opulence as the Supreme Personality of Godhead, but at the same time He is full of all renunciation. In the material world we find that one who has much opulence is not very much inclined to give it up, but Kṛṣṇa is not like this. He can renounce everything and remain complete in Himself.

When we read or study *Bhagavad-gītā* under a bona fide spiritual master we should not think that the spiritual master is presenting his own opinions. It is not he who is speaking. He is just an instrument. The real speaker is the Supreme Personality of Godhead, who is both within and without. At the beginning of His discourse on the *yoga* system in the Sixth Chapter of *Bhagavad-gītā*, Śrī Kṛṣṇa says,

anāśritaḥ karma-phalaṁ
kāryaṁ karma karoti yaḥ
sa sannyāsī ca yogī ca
na niragnir na cākriyaḥ

"One who is unattached to the fruits of his work and who works as he is obligated is in the renounced order of life, and he is the true mystic, not he who lights no fire and performs no work." (Bg. 6.1) Everyone is working and expecting some result. One may ask, What is the purpose of working if no result is expected? A remuneration or salary is always demanded by the worker. But here Kṛṣṇa indicates that one can work out of a sense of duty alone, not expecting the results of his activities. If one works in this way, then he is actually a *sannyāsī;* he is in the renounced order of life.

According to Vedic culture, there are four stages of life: *brahmacārī, gṛhastha, vānaprastha* and *sannyāsa. Brahmacārī* is student life devoted to training in spiritual understanding. *Gṛhastha* life is married householder life. Then upon reaching the approximate age of fifty, one may take the *vānaprastha* order—that is, he leaves his home and children and travels with his wife to holy places of pilgrimage. Finally he gives up both wife and children and remains alone to cultivate Kṛṣṇa consciousness, and that stage is called *sannyāsa*, or the renounced order of life. Yet Kṛṣṇa indicates that for a *sannyāsī*, renunciation is not all. In addition, there must be some duty. What then is the duty for a *sannyāsī*, for one who has renounced family life and no longer has material obligations? His duty is a most responsible one; it is to work for Kṛṣṇa. Moreover, this is the real duty for everyone in all stages of life.

In everyone's life there are two duties: one is to serve the illusion, and the other is to serve the reality. When one serves the reality, he is a real *sannyāsī*. And when one serves the illusion, he is deluded by *māyā*. One has to understand, however, that he is in all circumstances forced to serve. Either he serves the illusion or the reality. The constitutional position of the living entity is to be a servant, not a master. One may think that he is the master, but he is actually a servant. When one has a family he may think that he is the master of his wife, or his children, or his home, business and so on, but that is all false. One is actually the servant of his wife, of his children and of his business. The president may be considered the master of the country, but actually he is the servant of the country. Our position is always as servant—either as servant of the illusion or as servant of God. If, however, we remain the servant of the illusion, then our life is wasted. Of course everyone is thinking that he is not a servant, that he is working only for himself. Although the fruits of his labour are transient and illusory, they force him to become a servant of illusion, or a servant of his own senses. But when one awakens to his transcendental senses and actually becomes situated in knowledge, he then becomes a servant of the reality. When one comes to the platform of knowledge, he understands that in all circumstances he is a servant. Since it is not possible for him to be master, he is much better situated serving the reality instead of the illusion. When one becomes aware of this, he attains the platform of real knowledge. By *sannyāsa*, the renounced order of life, we refer to one who has come to this platform. *Sannyāsa* is a question of realization, not social status.

It is the duty of everyone to become Kṛṣṇa conscious and to serve the cause of Kṛṣṇa. When one actually realizes this he becomes a *mahātmā*, or a great soul. In *Bhagavad-gītā* Kṛṣṇa says that after many births, when one comes to the platform of real knowledge, he "surrenders unto Me." Why is this? *Vāsudevaḥ sarvam iti.* The wise man realizes that "Vāsudeva [Kṛṣṇa] is everything." However, Kṛṣṇa says that such a great soul is rarely found. Why is this? If an intelligent person comes to understand that the ultimate goal of life is to surrender unto Kṛṣṇa, why should he hesitate? Why not surrender immediately? What is the point in waiting for so many births? When one comes to that point of surrender, he becomes a real *sannyāsī.* Kṛṣṇa never forces anyone to surrender unto Him. Surrender is a result of love, transcendental love. Where there is force and where there is no freedom, there can be no love. When a mother loves a child, she is not forced to do so, nor does she do so out of expectation of some salary or remuneration.

Similarly, we can love the Supreme Lord in so many ways—we can love Him as master, as friend, as child or as husband. There are five basic *rasas*, or relationships, in which we are eternally related to God. When we are actually in the liberated stage of knowledge, we can understand that our relationship with the Lord is in a particular *rasa*. That platform is called *svarūpa-siddhi,* or real self-realization. Everyone has an eternal relationship with the Lord, either as master and servant, friend and friend, parent and child, husband and wife, or lover and beloved. These relationships are eternally present. The whole process of spiritual realization and the actual perfection of *yoga* is to revive our consciousness of this relationship. At present our relationship with the Supreme Lord is pervertedly reflected in this material world. In the material world, the relationship between master and servant is based on money or force or exploitation. There is no question of service out of love. The relationship between master and servant, pervertedly reflected, continues only for so long as the master can pay the servant. As soon as the payment stops, the relationship also stops. Similarly, in the material world there may be a relationship between friends, but as soon as there is a slight disagreement, the friendship breaks, and the friend becomes an enemy. When there is a difference of opinion between son and parents, the son leaves home, and the relationship is severed. The same with husband and wife; a slight difference of opinion, and there is divorce.

No relationship in this material world is actual or eternal. We must always remember that these ephemeral relationships are simply perverted reflections of that eternal relationship we have with the Supreme Personality of Godhead. We have experience that the reflection of an object in a glass is not real. It may appear real, but when we go to touch it we find that there is only glass. We must come to understand that these relationships as friend, parent, child, master, servant, husband, wife or lover are simply reflections of that relationship we have with God. When we come to this platform of understanding, then we are perfect in knowledge. When that knowledge comes, we begin to understand that we are servants of Kṛṣṇa and that we have an eternal love relationship with Him.

In this love relationship there is no question of remuneration, but of course remuneration is there, and it is much greater than whatever we earn here through the rendering of service. There is no limit to Śrī Kṛṣṇa's remuneration. In this connection there is the story of Bali Mahārāja, a very powerful king who conquered a number of planets. The denizens of the heavenly planets appealed to the Supreme Lord to save them, for they had been conquered by the demoniac king Bali Mahārāja. Upon hearing their pleas, Śrī Kṛṣṇa took the shape of a dwarf *brāhmaṇa* boy and approached Bali Mahārāja, saying, "My dear king, I would like something from you. You are a great monarch and are renowned for giving in charity to the *brāhmaṇas*, so would you give Me something?"

Bali Mahārāja said, "I will give You what You want."

"I simply want whatever land I can cover in three steps," the boy said.

"Oh, is that all?" the king replied. "And what will You do with such a small piece of land?"

"Though it may be small, it will suffice Me," the boy smiled.

Bali Mahārāja agreed, and the boy-dwarf took two steps and covered the entire universe. He then asked Bali Mahārāja where He was going to take His third step, and Bali Mahārāja, understanding that the Supreme Lord was showing him His favour, replied, "My dear Lord, I have now lost everything. I have no other property, but I do have my head. Would You so kindly step there?"

Lord Śrī Kṛṣṇa was then very much pleased with Bali Mahārāja, and He asked, "What would you like from Me?"

"I never expected anything from You," Bali Mahārāja said. "But I understand that You wanted something from me, and now I have offered You everything."

"Yes," the Lord said, "but from My side I have something for you. I shall remain always as an order-carrier servant in your court." In this way the Lord became Bali Mahārāja's doorman, and that was his return. If we offer something to the Lord, it is returned millions of times. But we should not expect this. The Lord is always eager to return the service of His servant. Whoever thinks that the service of the Lord is actually his duty is perfect in knowledge and has attained the perfection of *yoga*.

EIGHT

The Perfection of Yoga

IT IS A FACT, therefore, that in the progress of the living entity toward the perfection of *yoga*, birth in a family of *yogīs* or devotees is a great boon, for such a birth gives one special impetus.

prayatnād yatamānas tu
yogī saṁśuddha-kilbiṣaḥ
aneka-janma-saṁsiddhas
tato yāti parāṁ gatim

"But when the *yogī* engages himself with sincere endeavour in making further progress, being washed of all contaminations, then ultimately, after many, many births of practice, he attains the supreme goal." (Bg. 6.45) When one is finally freed from all contaminations, he attains the supreme perfection of the *yoga* system—Kṛṣṇa consciousness. Absorption in Kṛṣṇa is the perfect stage, as Kṛṣṇa Himself confirms:

bahūnāṁ janmanām ante
jñānavān māṁ prapadyate
vāsudevaḥ sarvam iti
sa mahātmā sudurlabhaḥ

"After many births and deaths, he who is actually in knowledge surrenders unto Me, knowing Me to be the cause of all causes and all that is. Such a great soul is very rare." (Bg. 7.19) Thus after many lifetimes of executing pious activities, when one becomes freed from all contaminations arising from illusory dualities, he engages in the transcendental service of the Lord. Śrī Kṛṣṇa concludes His discourse on this subject in this way:

yoginām api sarveṣāṁ
mad-gatenāntarātmanā
śraddhāvān bhajate yo māṁ
sa me yuktatamo mataḥ

"And of all *yogīs,* he who always abides in Me with great faith, worshipping Me in transcendental loving service, is most intimately united with Me in *yoga* and is the highest of all." (Bg. 6.47)

It therefore follows that the culmination of all *yogas* lies in *bhakti-yoga,* the rendering of devotional service unto Kṛṣṇa. Actually, all of the *yogas* delineated in *Bhagavad-gītā* end on this note, for Kṛṣṇa is the ultimate destination of all the *yoga* systems. From the beginning of *karma-yoga* to the end of *bhakti-yoga* is a long way to self-realization. *Karma-yoga*, without fruitive results, is the beginning of this path. When *karma-yoga* increases in knowledge and renunciation, the stage is called *jñāna-yoga*, or the *yoga* of knowledge. When *jñāna-yoga* increases in meditation on the Supersoul by different physical processes, and the mind is on Him, it is called *aṣṭāṅga-yoga*. And, when one surpasses *aṣṭāṅga-yoga* and comes to worship the Supreme Personality of Godhead, Kṛṣṇa, that is called *bhakti-yoga*, the culmination. Factually, *bhakti-yoga* is the ultimate goal, but to analyse *bhakti-yoga* minutely one has to understand the other processes. The *yogī* who is progressive is therefore on the true path to eternal good fortune. One who sticks to a particular point and does not make further progress is called by that particular name—*karma-yogī, jñāna-yogī, dhyāna-yogī, rāja-yogī, haṭha-yogī*, etc.—but if one is fortunate enough to come to the point of *bhakti-yoga*, Kṛṣṇa consciousness, it is to be understood that he has surpassed all the other *yoga* systems.

Kṛṣṇa consciousness is the last link in the yogic chain, the link that binds us to the Supreme Person, Lord Śrī Kṛṣṇa. Without this final link, the chain is practically useless. Those who are truly interested in the perfection of the *yoga* process should immediately take to Kṛṣṇa consciousness by chanting Hare Kṛṣṇa, understanding *Bhagavad-gītā*, and rendering service to Kṛṣṇa through this society for Kṛṣṇa consciousness and thereby surpass all other systems and attain the ultimate goal of all *yoga*— love of Kṛṣṇa.

* * *

Centres of the International Society for Krishna Consciousness

Founder-*Ācārya:* His Divine Grace A. C. Bhaktivedanta Swami Prabhupāda

For further information on classes, programmes, festivals, residential courses, and local meetings, please contact the centre nearest you.
✦ *Temples with restaurants or dining*

UNITED KINGDOM AND IRELAND

Belfast, Northern Ireland — 140 Upper Dunmurray Lane, Belfast BT17 0HE; Tel. +44-28-90620530; belfast@iskcon.org.uk; www.iskcon.org.uk/belfast

Birmingham, England — 84 Stanmore Road, Edgebaston, Birmingham B16 9TB; Tel. +44-121-4204999; birmingham@iskcon.org.uk; www.iskconbirmingham.org

Cardiff, Wales — The Soul Centre, 116 Cowbridge Road East, Canton, Cardiff, CF11 9DX; Tel. +44-2920-390391; the.soul.centre@pamho.net; www.thesoulcentre.net

Coventry, England — Kingfield Road, Radford, Coventry, West Midlands; (mail: 19 Gloucester Street, Coventry, CV1 3BZ); Tel. +44-24-76552822 or 5420; coventry@iskcon.org.uk; www.iskcon.org.uk/coventry

✦ **Dublin, Ireland** — 83 Middle Abbey Street, Dublin 1; Tel. +353-1-8729775; dublin@krishna.ie; www.krishna.ie

Lanarkshire, Scotland — Karuna Bhavan, Bankhouse Road, Lesmahagow, Lanarkshire, ML11 0ES; Tel. +44-1555-894790; Fax +44-1555-894526; karunabhavan@aol.com; www.iskcon.org.uk/scotland

Leicester, England — 21 Thoresby Street, North Evington, Leicester LE5 4GU; Tel. +44-116-2762587; leicester@iskcon.org.uk; www.iskconleicester.org

✦ **London, England** (city) — 10 Soho Street, London W1D 3DL; Tel. +44-20-74373662; shop: 72870269; Govinda's Restaurant: 74374928; Fax +44-20-74391127; london@pamho.net; www.iskcon-london.org

London, England (south) — 42 Enmore Road, South Norwood, London SE25 5NG; Tel. +44-20-86564296; www.iskcon.org.uk/snorwood

Manchester, England — 20 Mayfield Road, Whalley Range, Manchester M16 8FT; Tel. +44-161-2264416; manchester@iskcon.org.uk; www.iskcon.org.uk/manchester

Newcastle, England — 304 Westgate Road, Newcastle-upon-Tyne, Tyne & Wear NE4 6AR; Tel. +44-191-2721911; newcastle@iskcon.org.uk; www.iskcon.org.uk/newcastle

✦ **Swansea, Wales** — 8 Craddock Street, Swansea SA1 3EN; Tel. +44-1792-468469; iskcon.swansea@pamho.net; restaurant: govindas.swansea@pamho.net; www.iskconwales.org

✦ **Watford, England** — Bhaktivedanta Manor, Dharam Marg, Hilfield Lane, Aldenham, near Watford, Herts WD25 8EZ; Tel. +44-1923-857244; Fax +44-1923-852896; bhaktivedanta.manor@pamho.net; for accommodations: accommodations.requests@pamho.net; www.krishnatemple.com

RURAL COMMUNITY

Upper Lough Erne, Northern Ireland (Govindadwipa) — Inis Rath Island, Derrylin, Co. Fermanagh BT92 9GN; Tel. +44-28-67721512; bbt@krishnaisland.com; www.krishnaisland.com

ADDITIONAL RESTAURANT

Dublin, Ireland — Govinda's, 4 Aungier Street, Dublin 2; Tel. +353-1-4750309; info@govindas.ie; www.govindas.ie

Hare Krishna meetings are held regularly in more than forty towns in the UK and Ireland. For more information, contact: ISKCON Reader Services, P.O. Box 730, Watford WD25 8ZE, UK; readerservices@pamho.net; www.iskcon.org.uk

OTHER COUNTRIES

Amsterdam, Netherlands — Van Hilligaertstraat 17, Amsterdam 1072 JX; Tel. +31-20-6751404; Fax +31-20-6751405; amsterdam@pamho.net

Berlin, Germany — Kastanienallee 3, 10435 Berlin Pankow, Prenzlauer Berg; Tel. +49-30-44357296; Fax +49-30-48494074; harekrishna-berlin@pamho.net; www.krsna-is-cool.de

Brihuega, Spain (New Vraja Mandala) — (Santa Clara) 19411 Brihuega; Tel. +34-949-280436

Budapest, Hungary — Lehel u. 15-17, 1039 Budapest; Tel. +36-1-3910435; Fax +36-1-2423233; budapest@pamho.net; www.haribol.hu

✦ **Cologne, Germany** — Taunusstrasse 40, 51105 Köln; Tel. +49-221-8303778; restaurant: +49-221-9750323; Fax +49-221-8370485; iskcon.koeln@pamho.net; www.krishna-tempel.de

Copenhagen, Denmark — Skjulhøj Allé 44, 2720 Vanløse; Tel. +45-48-286446; Fax +45-48-287331; iskcon.denmark@pamho.net

Durban, South Africa — 50 Bhaktivedanta Swami Circle, Unit 5 (mail: P.O. Box 56003), Chatsworth 4030; Tel. +27-31-4033328; Fax +27-31-4034429; iskcon.durban@pamho.net

✦ **Durbuy, Belgium** (Radhadesh) — Château de Petite Somme, 6940 Septon-Durbuy; Tel. +32-86-322926; radhadesh@pamho.net; www.radhadesh.com

Florence, Italy (Villa Vrindavan) — via Scopeti 108, 50026 San Casciano in Val di Pesa (FI); Tel. +39-055-820054; Fax +39-055-828470; isvaripriya@libero.it

Helsinki, Finland — Ruoholahdenkatu 24 D (III krs) 00180 Helsinki; Tel. +358-9-6949879; Fax +358-9-6949837; harekrishna@harekrishna.fi; www. harekrishna.fi

Leipzig, Germany — Stöckelstrasse 60, 04347 Leipzig; Tel. +49-34-12348055; sadbhuja@gmx.net; www.krsna-is-cool.de

✦ **Los Angeles, USA** — 3764 Watseka Avenue, 90034; Tel. +1-310-836-2676; Fax +1-310-839-2715; nirantara@juno.com; restaurant: arcita@webcom.com

✦ **Mayapur, India** — Shree Mayapur Chandrodaya Mandir, P.O. Shree Mayapur Dham, Nadia District, W.B. 741 313; Tel. +91-3472-245239; Fax +91-3472-245238; mayapur.chandrodaya@pamho.net

✦ **Mumbai (Bombay), India** — Hare Krishna Land, Juhu 400 049; Tel. +91-22-26206860 Fax +91-22-26205214; iskcon.juhu@pamho.net; www.iskconmumbai.com

✦ **New Delhi, India** — Hare Krishna Hill, Sant Nagar Main Road, East of Kailash, 110 065; Tel. +91-11-26235133; Fax +91-11-26215421; delhi@pamho.net, guesthouse: neel.sunder@pamho.net

New York, USA — 305 Schermerhorn Street, Brooklyn, New York 11217; Tel. +1-718-855-6714; Fax +1-718-875-6127; ramabhadra@aol.com

Somogyvámos, Hungary — New Vraja-dhama, Fö út. 38., 8699 Somogyvámos; Tel./fax +36-85-340185; krisna-volgy@pamho.net; www.krisna-volgy.hu

✦ **Stockholm, Sweden** (city) — Fridhemsgatan 22, 11240 Stockholm; Tel. +46-8-6549002; Fax +46-8-6508813; info@harekrishnastockholm.com; www.harekrishnastockholm.com

Stockholm, Sweden (country) — Radha-Krishna Temple, Korsnäs Gård, 14792 Grödinge; Tel. +46-8-53029800; Fax +46-8-53025062; info@pamho.net; www.krishna.se

Sydney, Australia — 180 Falcon Street, North Sydney, NSW 2060 (mail: P.O. Box 459, Cammeray, NSW 2062); Tel. +61-2-99594558; Fax +61-2-99571893; info@iskcon.com.au; www.iskcon.com.au

✦ **Vrindavan, India** — Krishna-Balaram Mandir, Bhaktivedanta Swami Marg, Raman Reti, Mathura District, 281124; Tel. +91-565-2540021; Fax +91-565-2540053; vrindavan@pamho.net

Zurich, Switzerland — Bergstrasse 54, 8032 Zürich; Tel. +41-1-2623388; Fax +41-1-2623114; kgs@pamho.net; www.krishna.ch

This is a partial list of centres. For a full list, please contact one of the above addresses or visit us on the web at www.iskcon.com or www.krishna.com.